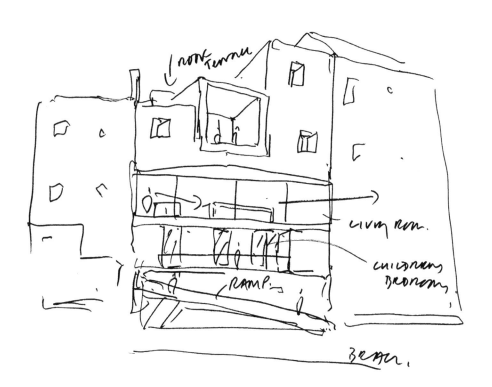

Making Space for Architecture

It is a common misconception to think that architecture originates from a sketch on a napkin. The design process of architecture, in particular of built architecture, differs significantly from the prevalent perception of how art is produced. Just like an artist tries to cross boundaries, the architect tries to love boundaries. Architectural design is to project what the existing could be. The existing is many things: the place, its boundaries, the architectural task, the building regulations, the money, the people who design, the people who build, the people who use and reside in the building and those who own it. The idea of what might be does not only have to consider the possibilities and boundaries of the place and the budget, but also the notions of all these people. It is extremely difficult to build a house that the client cannot imagine. Architecture does not originate from a sketch on a napkin, but within a collective space of imagination, which in some sense represents a section of our society and culture. In order for an architectural practice to produce good architecture, a design culture must exist, which encompasses both the office culture and the project culture. In our experience we have found that whoever wants to build good architecture, must acknowledge above all a cultural sphere of imagination, in which the people involved can concertedly unfold their power of imagination. Designing architecture primarily means making space for architecture. Architectural design means building space for the people, for their life and for their thoughts.

David Chipperfield Architects

Philip Jodidio

DAVID CHIPPERFIELD ARCHITECTS

1985

TASCHEN

Illustration page 1: Sketch of Private House in Corrubedo, Galicia, Spain. It shows the insertion of the new house into the alignment of existing structures.
Illustration page 4: Sketch of the James Simon Gallery, Museum Island, Berlin, Germany

© 2015 TASCHEN GmbH
Hohenzollernring 53, D–50672 Köln
www.taschen.com

ISBN 978–3–8365–5181–6
Printed in Slovakia

Editor: Florian Kobler, Berlin
Design: Birgit Eichwede, Cologne
Editorial coordintation: Inga Hallsson, Berlin
Collaboration: Harriet Graham, Turin, and Nina Helten/David Chipperfield Architects, Berlin
Production: Ute Wachendorf, Cologne

To stay informed about TASCHEN and our upcoming titles, please subscribe to our free magazine at www.taschen.com/magazine, follow us on Twitter, Instagram, and Facebook, or e-mail your questions to contact@taschen.com.

Contents

The Triumphant Modesty
of David Chipperfield

Apparently austere and rigorous, the architecture of David Chipperfield represents a real quest to reconcile the public with modernity through the coherence and materiality of its expression. Whether working in the complex ruins of the Neues Museum in Berlin or in the desert near Khartoum, this architect demonstrates that our time can, indeed, bring something original and powerful to the built environment. David Chipperfield took the time to speak at length to the author—the quotes reproduced here are from a conversation that took place in Berlin in January 2014. This brief overview is followed by a nearly verbatim part of the interview itself.

A look at the career of important architects often reveals that they worked, subsequent to their education, in the offices of one or more major figures of their profession. David Chipperfield, born in London in 1953, is no exception to this rule. He studied at the Kingston School of Art and received his Diploma in Architecture from the Architectural Association (AA, London, 1977). He then worked in the offices of Norman Foster and Richard Rogers, before establishing David Chipperfield Architects (London, 1985). The high-tech exuberance of both these masters was not to be the style of Chipperfield. Although a part of his career has been devoted to smaller projects—such as the Wagamama Restaurant (London, UK, 1996) or shops for the Dolce & Gabbana fashion brand (beginning in 1999)—David Chipperfield has more recently stepped in a broad way onto the international architecture scene with the completion of such works as the Museum of Modern Literature (Marbach, Germany, 2002–06), the America's Cup Building "Veles e Vents" (Valencia, Spain, 2005–06), and the Neues Museum (Berlin, Germany, 1997–2009). He has also completed buildings in the United States in such varied places as Des Moines (Des Moines Public Library, Des Moines, Iowa, 2002–06), Anchorage (Anchorage Museum at Rasmuson Center, Anchorage, Alaska, 2003–09), and St. Louis (Saint Louis Art Museum, St. Louis, Missouri, 2005–13).

Chipperfield's work on the Museum Island in Berlin is an ongoing project, as is his design for the San Michele Cemetery in Venice (Italy, 1998–). Both of these commitments concern historic places that have suffered with time and events, and, judging from the results thus far, it would appear that David Chipperfield fully masters the art of integrating modernity in a historically charged environment. One might be tempted to call his work "minimal" in its often rectilinear austerity, but his approach is more complex than that. In a recently published interview, the architect stated: "I suppose that we tend to look for a certain anonymous quality. I suppose I have an aversion to buildings that are telling you all the time how clever the architect is... I am interested in a sort of ordinariness as well as things being special. I really enjoy that edge between ordinariness and specialness, which is not easy to get." Perhaps even more to the point, he also stated: "I am interested in making buildings which have their own integrity..."[1]

Giving Value to Architectural Culture

In 2009, David Chipperfield was awarded the Order of Merit of the Federal Republic of Germany, the highest tribute paid to individuals for service to the nation. In 2011, he received the RIBA Royal Gold Medal, and, in 2013, the Praemium Imperiale, confirming the international reach of his reputation and realizations. As Director of the Venice Biennale's 13th International Architecture Exhibition in 2012, David Chipperfield explained: "The emphasis of the 2012 Biennale is on what we have in common. Above all, the ambition of 'Common Ground' is to reassert the existence of an architectural culture, made up not just of singular talents but a rich continuity of diverse ideas united in a common history, common ambitions, and common predicaments and ideals." Surely expressing his own feelings about the past, present, and future of architecture, he went on to write: "Layers of explicit and subliminal material form our memories and shape our judgments. While we struggle to orient ourselves in a continuously changing world, what we are familiar with is an inevitable part of our ability to understand our place. It is critical that our expectations and our history don't become a justification for sentimentality or resistance to progress. We must, therefore, articulate better our evaluations and prejudices if we are not to regard what has come before as something to escape and if we are to give value to a cumulative and evolving architectural culture rather than a random flow of meaningless images and forms."

David Chipperfield's career began auspiciously in Japan, with three projects. For one of these, Toyota Auto Kyoto (Kyoto, 1989–90, page 26), he was helped and influenced by Tadao Ando. Significantly, this project shows a real effort to respond to the apparently chaotic urban environment of modern Japan. Comparing a glass-block grid

Gormley Studio, London, UK, 2001–03
View of the enclosed courtyard and the main façade

If not otherwise indicated, all quotes come from the interviews with David Chipperfield by the author in Berlin in January 2014.

1   David Chipperfield, quoted in *El Croquis* 150, "David Chipperfield, 2006–2010," Madrid, 2010.

**Private House in Corrubedo,
Galicia, Spain, 1996–2002**
View out to sea from the living area

to traditional Japanese shoji screens, and employing white Kyoto plaster and pale Japanese oak, Chipperfield was beginning to ask questions about modernity and context that would form his later career. Another early work is the Private House in Berlin (Germany, 1994–96, page 28). The architect comments on both this project and the Japanese work: "The Private House in Berlin was one of our first projects in Germany. I remember trying to understand what I should do as an English architect in Kyoto: am I building an English building; am I coming to terms with what contemporary Japanese architects are doing and trying to catch up with them? Tadao Ando was a great influence, but I tried to find those things that seem to be beyond specific concerns and to look for the more general, the more physical and the more spatial. If you are in another country and you can't speak the language, you have to make signs. You have to keep things very simple and you have to get to the point. Those early buildings were clearly riffs on Modernism, in a way, and struggled with what a building in Japan should look like or what a building in Berlin should look like. Then you go to Miesian brick houses and you think about the courtyard house, or the brick villa of Mendelsohn."

An Autonomous Position

Until recent years, David Chipperfield's career has been marked most by his projects outside of England, and in particular in Germany. One early exception was the River & Rowing Museum (Henley-on-Thames, UK, 1989–97, page 30), in which he attempted to "merge figure and abstraction" in a most successful way. Again, his personal appreciation of the project is quite revealing as to his subsequent approach and work: "For the River & Rowing Museum I was back in England and smack in the middle of a very conservative environment in which everyone hated modern architecture. Prince Charles was very vocal at that time and the planning officer told me to consider whether Prince Charles would like our building. I questioned whether this was meant to be the basis of planning law in our country! I am fond of the River & Rowing Museum because it made me take very seriously the concerns of a community which was saying 'architects have been dumping bad architecture on us for the past 20 years, and we don't trust them anymore.' I felt at the time that if I designed a project with a flat roof it would not be built; but in 1989, it was quite difficult for a self-respecting modern architect to use a pitched roof. In the end it sort of hit both levels—Prince Charles did declare that he liked the building, it was his 'favorite building' of that year according to one of his advisors; but it was also short-listed for the Mies van der Rohe Prize. The project was a response to the idea that you have to take the resistance of a community seriously. The idea that we as architects should not be foisting architecture on society, working out strategies to get things built faster before the public can object. I think it was very nice how it became a popular building and if any project set me off, it was that one. From that point on, we have had a consistent philosophical approach—the idea of finding an autonomous position that makes sense and has meaning."

A different example of contextual response occurs with the Private House in Corrubedo (Galicia, Spain, 1996–2002, page 32), which is located on the waterfront on Spain's northwestern Atlantic coast. The architect succeeds here both in integrating the house into what appears to be a hodgepodge of different structures along the harbor and, at the same time, in creating an obviously new and exciting form. The house represents an intriguing combination of contextual integration with affirmed modernity. Chipperfield refers to the context here as "a fishing village with a number of

Des Moines Public Library,
Des Moines, Iowa, USA, 2002–06
Southeast elevation

equally ugly provisional buildings." But he says: "People like it there because it sort of fits in and yet it doesn't fit in. It is clearly a visitor, but a respectful one." Illustrating the continuity of his thinking and process, Chipperfield has made a similar contextual response in the case of his much more recent Joachimstrasse campus in Berlin (Germany, 2007–13, page 84). Intended on the street side as his own residence and within as a group of buildings for his offices, the project clearly fits into the scale of its rather unattractive street environment, while immediately setting a different rhythm. "When you look at the façades," says David Chipperfield, "we put three levels in instead of four, and six windows instead of 32, but otherwise it is very contextual. In school we were always told that in order to be contextual, windows have to line up, but I don't think that is necessarily true." Referring to both Corrubedo and Joachimstrasse, he says: "These buildings are highly contextual but they don't actually line up with anything."

A Place More Than a Building

The Gormley Studio (London, UK, 2001–03, page 34) represents an effort to take a very basic shedlike form and to make it invest its space in a material way. "Antony (Gormley) wanted very simple space with top light," says David Chipperfield. "He also wanted a big space in the front as a place to work, because he works outside a lot. It is a forecourt and it meant that the building had no relation to the street. I was nervous about that. So I persuaded him to put the stairs outside. That means that if you go from downstairs to upstairs, you always have to go into the courtyard. Therefore the stairs belong to this space as well as the building." Both in the words he chooses to explain his gestures and in the final form of his architecture, David Chipperfield seeks to be clear, to make gestures that have a meaning and are not merely aesthetic statements. He is also clearly concerned with what he again and again calls materiality, in this instance employing the very visible galvanized steel stairways in the way he describes. Significantly, the Gormley Studio also "reflects the large-scale, industrial-architectural vernacular of the surrounding buildings."

David Chipperfield's analysis of projects is clearly related to context but also to physicality—how materials are used and what they express. He is quite frank in assessing the challenges and responses to given buildings. In the case of the Des Moines Public Library (Des Moines, Iowa, USA, 2002–06, page 36), he explains: "This was a competition we won to design a structure with an incredibly low budget. I can say it was the cheapest building I ever built. Obviously you can't put a sign on the completed building explaining the circumstances, but you can influence where you set your idea. Before, there was a civic museum here with steps and columns and nobody went to it. This was an initiative to make the library more public, so we put it in a park. The concept was that because it was a glass building, even though you might be reading books and cut off, you could always be in the city and see the city. It has been very successful and everyone likes it. It is a very approachable building, which was our main concern— how to make a library a public building. It is a glass building for construction reasons, but with some materiality because it has a copper mesh between the two layers of glass. It gives a sense of materiality even if it is sort of prepacked."

There is frequent reference in architectural theory to the sense of place, whereas modern architecture has repeatedly neglected its environment to focus on often extravagant forms. Chipperfield, on the contrary, has tried to extend a number of his buildings so that they become inviting places to be. Explaining the Museum of Modern Literature (Marbach am Neckar, Germany, 2002–06, page 38), he says: "Marbach really helped us in Germany. It is hallowed ground, the birthplace of Friedrich Schiller. After World War II, literature was one of the things that Germany could hold on to as part of

Museum of Modern Literature, Marbach, Germany, 2002–06
The museum is located on top of a rock plateau overlooking the valley of the Neckar River

its rebuilding, its spirit and identity. Marbach became an important destination for any-body working with German literature, but was less known to the general public. Our client wanted to offer something to a wider audience. It was an interesting site, where our building had to negotiate two levels, and we made a kind of small temple. As an object it confirms the existing square, and also makes a sort of *mirador*, a place to be. Who, aside from a specialist, is going to just go into a dark room and look at manu-scripts? We nearly doubled the size of the building with these terraces and colonnades. There is an attempt to integrate it with the landscape and make a place more than a building."

The idea of making "a place more than a building" is a recurring one in David Chip-perfield's work. As he says: "In the case of the America's Cup Building (Valencia, Spain, 2005–06, page 42), the same thing happened. The program was for a VIP building that would sit in the harbor; a place where people would go with a security badge to watch all the boats going in and out. But the mayor also wanted this to become the symbol of the expansion of the city to the sea. I thought, how can the building become a sym-bol for the city if access is restricted to those with VIP tickets? It was also clear that visi-tors wouldn't want to watch boates from inside a glass building. Therefore, instead of just adding a balcony, we started the other way around—why not make a series of balconies and then put some rooms inside? People without badges can walk through the first floor, even if they are not allowed to go to the upper two floors. In this instance, it is precisely the non-programmatic space that everyone likes. The inside spaces are just meeting rooms and places to watch TV."

Chipperfield's role in creating spaces for social interaction has on occasion been equally proactive, as was the case in the headquarters for BBC Scotland at Pacific Quay (Glasgow, UK, 2001–07, page 44). The organization of the structure around a central atrium seems to be an "obvious" architectural gesture, but, in fact, Chipperfield in-vented it for very specific reasons, not really related to the formal aspects of space. "The BBC is an office building containing an apparently useless space that became its most useful space," he states. "The concept was based on the way radio programs are made, with certain people working in offices and others sitting in big boxes making

America's Cup Building "Veles e Vents", Valencia, Spain, 2005–06
An overall view of the structure with its staggered slab design

BBC Scotland at Pacific Quay,
Glasgow, UK, 2001–07
Tiered steps, platforms and terraces crafted from
local red sandstone in the central atrium

recordings. The client had imagined two buildings. I thought this was a bit dull and suggested that the recording studios could be in the middle so that everyone involved, throughout the institution, would feel somehow connected to the production process. Those boxes are different sizes, situated in an atrium that connects everything and becomes a social space. Useless space that becomes key to the project—this is a recurring idea." Once again, the architect's very simple and direct way of explaining his motivations and the net result of his intervention is striking and comprehensible even to the person who is relatively uninterested in the craft of architecture. He is not seeking architectural effect so much as to fulfill the requirements of the given project, and, if possible, to enlarge the periphery of what seems to be possible.

Retaining the Original Material

It seems clear that, to date, the most highly visible of David Chipperfield's projects has been the reconstruction of the Neues Museum in Berlin (Germany, 1997–2009, page 50). Set in the heart of Berlin, actually in the former Eastern zone, the Museum Island, on which the Neues Museum is set, has become the architect's most prestigious and perhaps complex ongoing project, since he continues to work there. Designed by

Friedrich August Stüler (1841–59), the Neues Museum was heavily damaged during World War II. The practice states: "The key aim of the project was to recomplete the original volume, and encompassed the repair and restoration of the parts that remained after the destruction of World War II. The original sequence of rooms was restored, with new building sections that create continuity with the existing structure." As Norman Foster did perhaps to a lesser extent in the Reichstag, Chipperfield chose to carry out a restoration that left visible some of the scars of war. His own explanation of the project makes clear his motivations: "It wasn't about retaining the damage; it was about retaining the original material. Take a wall with scars in the plaster work—one method would be to remove the damaged plaster and redo it. Our approach was that no original material could be removed allied to the idea that the difference between the old and the new should only be perceptible in a second glance. This is how archeological repair is done: you don't confuse the repair with the original. There was a lot of rhetoric about us wanting to make a monument to war, but that was not at all the idea. We took a much more secular attitude toward the ruin: the important thing was the original material, which we refused to discard. If you were working on a 15th-century Italian church you would adopt the same approach, you wouldn't even think twice about it."

As might be the case of a number of other famous architects, David Chipperfield has completed several prestigious museum projects, aside from the Neues Museum. Another German case is that of the Folkwang Museum (Essen, 2007–10, page 64). Here, as elsewhere, Chipperfield was called on in a sense to reconcile a historic location with a real sense of modernity. "At the Folkwang Museum we designed an addition to the museum to replace an existing structure" he states. "The original building was bombed out, as the whole of Essen was. In 1981, there was a new extension built that was soon considered inadequate. Years later they decided to knock it down. The question was: how to replace it with another modern building that didn't make the same mistakes." Here the problem was somehow less the damage of war than it was the challenge of proving that architecture of quality still exists.

**Folkwang Museum,
Essen, Germany, 2007–10**
Foyer, view into an internal courtyard

**Saint Louis Art Museum,
St. Louis, Missouri, USA, 2005–13**
Gallery space with floor-to-ceiling windows
providing views of the surrounding landscape

Very Successful and Very Modest

The architect has successfully approached museum projects where contemporary art and thus living artists are involved. "An interesting thing is that artists and curators are really supportive of our work," says David Chipperfield. "Folkwang Museum was very well received by the art world, as were The Hepworth Wakefield and Turner Contemporary. If an institution has good spaces then artists will want to show their work in this environment, which is hugely important. Artists often hate showing work in museums for very good reasons. We have clients who are happy because artists are attracted to their exhibition spaces." And yet the commitment of the architect to such ideas as the materiality and meaning of his work, often expressed in forms that are not outwardly spectacular, has not always brought him waves of support. He cites the example of the Saint Louis Art Museum (St. Louis, Missouri, USA, 2005–13, page 80): "The project is an extension to the existing Saint Louis Art Museum; it is modest but very successful. The American architectural community has largely ignored it because America is now used to every museum extension being a novelty. Saint Louis hasn't upset anybody, it isn't talked about but for art, I think these are some of the nicest spaces we have done. The top light is stunning."

Like his earlier project in Corrubedo and his home and office in Berlin on the Joachimstrasse, David Chipperfield's work on the Kaufhaus Tyrol Department Store (Innsbruck, Austria, 2007–10, page 66) demonstrates his ability to fundamentally reconcile tradition, or a complex site, with his specific idea of modernity, which, as he explains, may owe as much to Mies and Corbu as to Ando and Siza. He states: "Kaufhaus Tyrol is interesting because we had to deliver a very strong physical project in a historic and sensitive setting. It is a huge commercial project in the middle of a historic center, so it was a question of scale to make this façade fit in. We did it by trying to get some complexity and depth into the façade. What I quite like about it is that it is a commercial project that delivers a certain architectural integrity. This was slightly forced on the client in this instance by the sensitivity of the site." And so, even the commercial clients that David Chipperfield finds overtly committed to financial gain are made to come around to his point of view, not an insignificant accomplishment in these times of unbridled capitalism. Nor has David Chipperfield been lacking for institutional clients. He was selected early in 2015 to develop a new design for the Southwest Wing for modern and contemporary art at the Metropolitan Museum of Art in New York. His work is full of the sense and sensitivity that is apparent in his own words. He succeeds in building with as much simplicity and directness as he employs in his explanation of his motivations and work. There is a kind of triumphant modesty in the work of David Chipperfield.

David Chipperfield in Conversation with the Author in Berlin

Philip Jodidio Do you have a sense of coming home now that you are building more in the United Kingdom than you did in the past? The question also has to do with the reasons for which you may have built more abroad than in your own country.

David Chipperfield Britain is not the easiest place to be an architect. I think that most architects feel that it is difficult to establish yourself and that this has been the case for some time. Even the architects that we know as British—such as Norman Foster, Richard Rogers or Zaha Hadid—none of them really established themselves in Britain. Nor would Zaha Hadid regard herself as being well located by her work in Britain. Some, like Michael Hopkins, Nick Grimshaw or Terry Farrell, have found enough work at home, and they have been reasonably successful abroad as well; but it has not been easy for anyone in the past 20 years to build their career in the UK. The dominant architectural culture in Britain is a commercial one. Public projects are few and far between; there is not much of a public system for housing or schools, for example, so I do not take my condition personally. I established my work chasing projects in diverse places. You don't assemble a portfolio by sitting in your office and waiting for the phone to ring; you have got to go out there and do it yourself. We designed and built the River & Rowing Museum (Henley-on-Thames, UK, 1989–97, page 30) 20 years ago and then there was a gap and, more recently, we completed two more, The Hepworth Wakefield (Wakefield, UK, 2003–11, page 72) and Turner Contemporary (Margate, UK, 2006–11, page 68). Both of these have become well-known and successful as cultural

**Am Kupfergraben 10 Gallery Building,
Berlin, Germany, 2003–07**
View from the "Eiserne Brücke"

projects, but neither was delivered by the state. They were private initiatives that managed to get funding through the public system. It is not like Germany where there is a publically funded cultural initiative. In Britain, you need a group of people who obsess with doing a museum in Wakefield and then chip away at it themselves. They must do a competition with no money to get the project sufficiently far advanced so that then particular kinds of grants from the government become available. There is never a moment when it feels like a public project.

You Only Get Employed If You Can Add Value

Q It sounds as though you are not very positive about the ongoing situation in England; nothing has changed really for you or for the system?

DC I think that what changes is that as one gets older commercial developers perceive greater potential for you to add value. Essentially, what has happened is that architects now have to justify the value they add. In the past, it was more generally accepted that good design or architecture, or a good plan, somehow made a better society. As we have shifted to a dominantly free market, the question is no longer whether you make a better society, but whether you make more money. The truth is that an architect is only employed if he can add value. An office like mine in London is not going to be employed just to produce a good commercial project and to make money out of it. It has to be because we have more chance of obtaining planning permission in a difficult situation or that we add a chance of the developer getting more square meters to sell them for a higher price. Today's architecture in the UK is unfortunately about adding value in a way that is quantifiable.

Q You spend a good deal of time in Berlin, and you have public work here as well as private: is there a great difference in the way the commissions are obtained?

DC Germany retains its idea of being a social democracy, even though it has been somewhat eroded. The public sector is not quite what it was 10 or 20 years ago and private investment is becoming more important. There are more projects in the city being initiated by the private sector than there would have been 15 years ago. There is, however, still an ethos and attitude that was formed by the idea of the state. Even when a private investor employs an architect in Germany, they tend to inherit some of the habits of the public system. In Britain, there is no recommended fee scale, there are no guidelines, whereas in Germany state guidelines still have some importance. In Berlin, there is a public structure and there are people employed by the city to consider urban development. In London, we don't have a city architect or a public works department—that has been privatized. Mrs. Thatcher felt the city to be a private commodity. Essentially, a developer in London buys a piece of land and sees how much he can get away with. The architect is then a tool by which the developer might say 'instead of building 10 stories, I think we can get 20.' In Berlin, there is a city plan, in London it is a wild horse. The deregulation is intended to make it as easy as possible for investment to happen. And clearly there has been a great deal of investment in London due to this situation.

What Are You Doing to the General Condition?

Q But there was criticism in Berlin too of the post-Wall development master plan that imposed so many restrictions...

DC I don't think anyone was totally comfortable with it. Hans Stimmann was a formidable figure. He insisted on a clear framework – perhaps ideologically too strongly – but at least it established an a priori condition. It was something that people could work with or work against. What he said, and what I still agree with, is that the status of the city depends on its general form rather than on the quality of individual buildings. Ideally one would like a city that has a really good form and the form is made out

Joachimstrasse, Berlin, Germany, 2007–13
The practice's café and small restaurant, called *Kantine*, is located in the courtyard

of very good buildings. Rafael Moneo wrote a very nice text for the Biennale in 2012 about Milan. I wanted him to talk about the common ground of the city and he also said that he felt that the quality of architecture is less important than the quality of the city's form. Going around Milan, he realized how much architecture contributed to the reading of the city. The discussion has tended to become polarized. The period between 1990 and 2010 produced many singular buildings by figures like Jacques Herzog, Zaha Hadid, Daniel Libeskind, Frank Gehry or Rem Koolhaas. The opposite camp says that it is fine to engage with those buildings individually, but how do we engage with the general condition of the city?

Q You are in the camp that is more interested in the general condition?

DC Clearly what one would like is the perfect condition of the singular building being contextualized. So many new developments are a mess, but you can't blame buildings individually. It is the sum that is completely uninteresting.

Q Thus such situations are out of the control of any single architect.

DC One would hope that an architect's concern for making good architecture is reciprocated by society's concerns for making a good environment. But that mechanism, commitment, or even interest no longer exists. Architecture is left on its own. The architect is meant to solve these issues, therefore what we do is move our attention to the singular pieces. From these we can argue that perhaps architecture is not in such a bad condition. That would be fine if the world was made out of railway stations and museums and a few other special buildings, but walking around a city is about visiting shopping centers and taking the kids to school. Who is looking after that stuff? Architects are both powerful and powerless, lacking authority beyond the real physical task. That is our paradox. I think that every architect wants to believe that they do more than just make forms and run a business, or run a business making forms. Most good architects believe that by building they are contributing something substantial, not just a pile of architectural novelties. We all grew up with the ambitions of Modernism concerning the relationship between buildings and society. Architecture was socially grounded. It is quite frustrating if the potential of a project doesn't contain any of that. The thing that satisfies me most with this project (Joachimstrasse, Berlin, Germany, 2007–13, page 84) is not that we managed to build it from insulated concrete, but rather that on a nice day the courtyard is filled with people. Its social ambition is completely realized. Even in the snow it makes a difference to the lives of the 100 people who work here, and other people who come in from the outside. I find that completely satisfying.

Q And intentional?

DC Of course.

Q You have said: "If I thought architecture was nomadic and light-footed, it could be very interesting, but it's not true." I believe you were speaking to some extent about Norman Foster. I worked on a book with Renzo Piano who said at the outset that the book should be about "lightness and flight." This is an idea that you apparently reject. Do you feel that architecture must necessarily be rooted in the earth—do you contrast rootedness with lightness or flight?

Most Buildings Are Built Roughly the Same Way

DC I suppose I do. Most buildings are built roughly the same way. If we are talking about buildings that have any urban presence, anything over three floors, there is a substantial amount of work that has to go on under the ground to make these things stand up. However light a building might look on completion, six months into the construction process it is just a great hole with people digging mud out, looking roughly the same as it has for the past 500 years. Then concrete is poured into the foundations, followed by a structural frame which is either made of concrete or steel, and this frame is subsequently covered. That covering can either give the impression of lightness or it can give the impression of heaviness; both are rhetorical. We don't need to make buildings heavy anymore. It is not very economical to make load-bearing walls and punch holes into them. The easiest way is always to use a frame. Anything put within that frame is by definition reasonably lightweight, even if it assumes an image of heaviness. Creating an effect of lightness is surprisingly close in material terms to what is required to make a building look heavy. Thermally, we have to arrive roughly at the same place by one method or another.

Q In Berlin on Joachimstrasse, you have made a concrete building, have you not?

DC There is a tendency to describe buildings by the materiality of their exterior: this is a brick building, a steel building, a glass building. In reality they are all concrete or steel buildings with a skin. What is interesting about our office building is that we made it exclusively out of concrete. But that is actually counterintuitive.

Ordinarily, to build a concrete wall one must build two with a gap in between for insulation. It is expensive to do, and also very difficult. Here we forced it, so there is only one wall. But often when we say it is a concrete building, it is really covered with concrete cladding; when we say it is a brick building, it is often a brick cladding. The substance of things is much more difficult to describe in contemporary architecture, especially as it gets closer and closer to the pressures of production.

Less and Less Engaged in the Idea of Making Cities

Q You don't really have a choice in many buildings about how things are done in terms of construction then?

DC The problem for architects is that we are gradually being sidelined. We are sidelined socially because we are less and less engaged in the idea of making cities. In England at the moment, we need to build half a million housing units. There is no discussion about what form that housing might take, only about who is going to deliver them. There is no intellectual idea whatsoever. We are becoming isolated from the constructional process because the commercial pressures of delivery are becoming more important than architectural concerns. Every time you try to do something interesting, you are flying in the face of this ethos. However, the industry does not deliver good construction of its own accord; there would be little aesthetic satisfaction if constructors were left alone to put buildings together.

Q In Mexico City for the Museo Jumex (Mexico City, Mexico, 2009–13, page 76), you found a different situation, did you not?

DC Everyone warned us that we would have a nightmare in Mexico. It was actually one of the more enjoyable building processes because it was so engaged: the people doing the stone were a father-and-son team; the company that made the window frames produced them themselves. Everything was brought back to a rather "built" method—it was very logical with all the individuals playing the game. The major participants were engaged too—which is not often the case in the industry. Working with a construction company, one doesn't tend to have relationships with anyone connect-

Museo Jumex, Mexico City, Mexico, 2009–13
View of the museum and the surrounding public plaza

ed to the site. In Mexico it was quite nice—the whole thing was rather primitive in a positive sense. It was a strange experience to have the impression that you were building a building with builders.

The Physical Dimension

Q You have said: "I suppose we tend to look for a certain anonymous quality. I suppose I have an aversion to buildings that are telling you all the time how clever the architect is. I am interested in a sort of ordinariness as well as things being special. I really enjoy that edge between ordinariness and specialness which is not easy to get." Does the perception of that edge require a specific knowledge of architecture or is it something that the ordinary person who walks into the building should feel? Are you also referring to the edge between instinct and knowledge?

DC Yes. Also, experience and image. The problem in architecture increasingly is how to deliver something that has a physical dimension. It is much easier to be commissioned on an image than it is on an experience. Compare the architect who says "I know this proposal doesn't look amazing now, but it will be," to the one who says "this

Anchorage Museum at Rasmuson Center,
Anchorage, Alaska, USA, 2003–09
South façade

is how it is going to look, doesn't that look exciting?" Image wins over idea in the speculation of an architectural project. When it is delivered, it is a bit easier, but getting there is difficult. Architecture has components of representation, identity, language, and physical presence. As we have become less confident in architecture's quiet physical strengths, we tend to turn the volume up on its other potential, that is, on its rhetorical identity. There are some brilliant architects who have managed to put the two things together, but it tends to be a dialogue between what you can imagine and what you can deliver. I would argue that sometimes an architect's lack of imagination is partly due to his concern about how to deliver something. As one sketches, the worries about buildability can limit the imagination. If architects were just making models we wouldn't have those concerns. There is a relationship between what one tries to imagine, beyond what one has done before, and how one might deliver it. The way in which a building is built has a profound influence on its quality and I would argue that the physical and experiential dimensions of architecture can be more important than any other... or rather, should be more important.

Q The significance of the image of architecture has changed then?

DC We all make up our mind about buildings without even seeing them. It used to be that one would never pass judgment on a piece of architecture without seeing the real thing. Now we constantly judge buildings that we haven't seen. But you can probably get a better idea of a painting through a reproduction than you can with a building.

Q Is Álvaro Siza another architect who is on the edge between what you call ordinariness and specialness?

DC I think so. Even Siza is mortal, but he has a highly personal hand and yet he manages to somehow neutralize it within the intelligence of the project. There is something magical about Siza's ability to create a gesture that could be indulgent and very personal, and slightly willful or mannered, and to somehow embed it into an idea that seems to be much more general.

Q At the time of the end of your education in about 1978 you said that "instead of Mies and Corb, all of a sudden Asplund, Lewerentz, and Lutyens became much more significant to us." Today, would you cite these architects as being among those that still matter to you?

DC The 1970s were very confusing for architecture. For the first half of my architectural training, Modernism was still alive; at least it had not been killed off as effectively as it was a few years later. An architect's early diet consisted of the Modernist heroes: Le Corbusier, Aalto, Mies, Gropius. I had three years of that and then there was a big mood change at the end of the 1970s. While clearly there had been a dark cloud hanging over Modernism for a long time and it had lost its energy, things really changed with a new interest in history which then became known as Postmodernist architecture. At the AA (Architectural Association School of Architecture, London) there was a big Beaux-Arts exhibition followed by a wave of history lectures. Charles Jencks started to package this into a much more digestible format. Then people started looking at Lutyens, who had been completely out of bounds a few years before. Suddenly, everyone was interested in history. Then came an uncomfortable period in London when we started to see the results of this being built, which was enough to put you off history again. One realized that whilst this was an interesting moment intellectually, in terms of architectural production it was very disappointing. At that time in London there was the high-tech movement, with Foster, Rogers, Grimshaw, and Hopkins, but also the Postmodern group with architects such as Terry Farrell. They were two very distinct camps.

Q Today, haven't architects like Mies and Corb come back into your own thinking?

DC I don't think that they ever went away. Once they are in your blood... One can't go to Poissy and see the Villa Savoye as a 22-year-old student and not be completely bowled over by it. Life is never quite the same again for an architect. In Britain there aren't many Modernist buildings of such intensity.

There Is a Richness in Architecture

Q How does the word "minimal" strike your fancy? You refer to the integrity of a building, but there is also what I would call simplicity in your buildings. Is this apparent simplicity at all related to Minimalism? Is that an offensive word?

DC It is not offensive, but I don't think it really means much in terms of our work. I am interested in the idea of reducing and making explicit. I was brought up on Modernism and was a great believer. My faith was shaken when I realized that there was a richness to architecture which Modernism no longer represented. Modernism wasn't delivering the Villa Savoye anymore. It was creating horrible commercial projects in England and just about everywhere else. I was trying to sustain my belief but there wasn't much evidence on the ground. Then people said, go and look at Lutyens, look at Voysey and Philip Webb. These were architects who seemed to have had fun in their work, whereas late Modernism wasn't fun at all. Of course, when the Postmodern architects started to build their own idea of a new style there was little evidence to support that either.

Q What was the alternative then?

DC Wilfried Wang, who founded *9H* magazine with Nadir Tharani and then the *9H* Gallery with Ricky Burdett, introduced us to people like Snozzi, Siza, and Moneo—people who were making architecture. They hadn't lost their faith but were interested in making things that had a strong physical presence, which showed in a way that

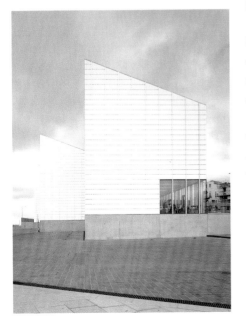

Turner Contemporary, Margate, UK, 2006–11
View of the mono-pitched volumes from the east

Modernism could survive. From that I became very convinced that the task for an architect was to ensure that the idea was evident. Architecture has to be self-explanatory. It requires total clarity, what one might call simplicity.

No Need for Radical Ambitions

Q And then you reach for the ordinary?

DC We have the opportunity as architects to make spaces and make objects. This is an opportunity that poets and painters lack but that sculptors like to aspire to. We have this particular opportunity and yet how often does one feel it in architecture? How often does one feel that the architect is actually in control of the physical, spatial elements in the way that a painter or a writer would be—that they have actually done these things on purpose? There is a condensation of the idea into a physical result. I think concentration can be read as a sort of simplicity, or the limitation and clarification of the ambition. The idea of the ordinary is a slightly different thing. It is trying to say that architecture's responsibility, in terms of what it delivers, can rest with those things. It doesn't have to assume all sorts of radical ambitions.

Q Perhaps theory is less useful than actually building?

DC Yes, there can be a lot of ideas in building itself. One can't just do good details, one can't make a building out of a series of window frames. What we look for is a certain integrity between an idea and its delivery. There must be balance in terms of a mastery of intellectual and physical skills; it is no use being expert at building and not knowing what one wants to build, or being full of ideas about what one might want to build and not knowing how. Experience of building can stimulate valid ideas about architecture. Equally, theory can be more closely related to the making of architecture than we want to admit. Architects' lives are complicated hugely by worrying about the way we build. We may have ideas, but how to persuade everyone else? Most clients would like to buy designs and get rid of the architect. That's what I would do if I were a commercial client. I would say, I have your name, I have the idea, but I am going to get someone else to build it. What I mean by this somewhat ironic tone is that we undervalue architecture, we undervalue its real qualities.

Making the Normal Special

Q When you received the Praemium Imperiale there were comments in the press about the influence of Japan on your work. The Japan Art Association pointed out that the idea of uniting modern architecture with traditional principles is an influence that you may have received in Japan. Is there a substantial influence of Japan in your work?

DC Absolutely. My first three buildings were in Japan. One was a homage to Tadao Ando, who helped me through the process of building there. The idea of making architecture physical, apparent, and evident is strong in Japan. I like the way the Japanese intensify normal things and give them more meaning. The idea of meaning is critical to what we do as architects. It is about trying to intensify experience, which the Japanese are very good at; they are almost fetishistic in their celebration of the seasons, for example.

Q Do you then accept the idea that Japan has influenced the references to tradition and modernity in your work?

DC Yes, it has influenced the importance of continuity. I think there is a respect for tradition and values but those values are very much grounded in the physical, or the

Neues Museum, Berlin, Germany, 1997–2009
Staircase Hall

ritual. Take for instance having a bath, having washed before getting in. We get in a bath to wash; the Japanese have a bath to experience and enjoy water. What could be more normal than water, but how beautiful that the water goes right up to the edge. One is not sitting in a vessel with water in it, but sitting in water that almost defines the vessel. Giving intensity to something very normal would seem to me a quality that one can pursue in architecture.

1989–90 ▸ Toyota Auto Kyoto

Kyoto, Japan

This 1410-square-meter building forms a strict rectangle in plan consisting of a gray concrete shell and a black stainless-steel inner volume that is visible from the outside at the uppermost of the three levels. The client, the Toyota Auto Kyoto Corporation, sought a multiuse facility "conceived and presented as if it were a private house." Indeed, the 10-meter concrete walls are erected close to traditional houses in the Higashiyama district. Higashiyama Ward is located in the east of the city between the Kamo River and the Higashiyama mountains, and is known as the location of Kiyo-mizu-dera Temple and the Gion tourist area. This was the second of three early 1990s projects carried out by the architect in Japan, along with the Gotoh Museum in Matsudo (Chiba, 1988–91) and the Matsumoto Corporation Headquarters (Okayama, 1990–92), both of which were also characterized by strict lines and concrete walls. The ground floor is used as a Toyota showroom along with a restaurant, while a bookshop and clothing store are set upstairs, and an apartment for entertaining clients is in the rooftop pavilion, which offers a view of the hills that surround the city. The architect emphasizes the effort made to respond to local context that consists in the usual narrow streets with an irregular accumulation of small buildings. A glass-block grid is compared to the traditional Japanese shoji screens, while white Kyoto plaster and pale Japanese oak also connect the structure to its urban and cultural environment.

Above:
The inward-looking lower levels are arranged around a shallow reflective pool

Opposite:
Exterior circulation routes allowing direct access to each space

Right:
Concept sketch

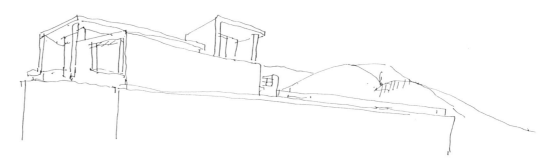

1994–96 ▸ Private House in Berlin

Berlin, Germany

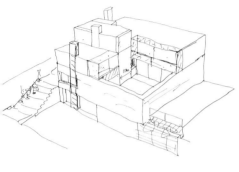

Above:
Concept sketch

Opposite:
Stairway leading to the main entrance

Right:
Rear of the house with the sunken garden and recessed glazing, opening in broad rectangular swathes

This large residence (1450 m²) is located in southwestern Berlin. The architects refer to the "early Modernist houses of Erich Mendelsohn and Mies van der Rohe, especially the latter's three projects of the late 1920s: Wolf, Esters, and Lange." The Wolf House (Gubin, Poland, 1925–27) was based on the earlier unbuilt design for a Brick Country House (1923). The Esters and Lange Houses (1928–30) are located next to each other in Krefeld (Germany). They are clad in brick with a steel load-bearing structure, and do, indeed, bear comparison to this private house in Berlin, though the apparent opacity of the brick surfaces is greater in the more recent residence. A south-facing courtyard opens into a generous garden. Recessed steel-framed windows seem to be carved out of the solid façade, contrasting with the flat brick surfaces. Despite the apparent strictness and relatively closed appearance of the structure, the architect makes numerous connections between interior and exterior and also plays on interior ceiling heights, referring to an "interplay between abstract space and domestic program." As is often the case in Chipperfield's work, the planar interplay of exterior forms is clearly echoed in the plans of the house.

1989–97 ▸ River & Rowing Museum

Henley-on-Thames, UK

Located in Mill Meadows, the River & Rowing Museum was officially opened in 1998 by Queen Elizabeth II. The town's only museum is largely devoted to rowing, of which Henley is a recognized center, hosting such events as the Henley Royal Regatta, or the Olympic rowing in 1908 and 1948. The museum has a collection of rowing boats, and it is intended to provide documentation on the sport, the Thames, and the town itself. The architects explain: "The earliest sketches for the museum at Henley-on-Thames were inspired by local river boathouses and the traditional wooden barns of Oxford-shire—a simple and clear architectural idea that makes natural associations with the surrounding area." The long, interconnected rectangular structures, with a gross floor area of 2300 square meters, have concrete or glass bases, but are largely clad in untreated green oak, with pitched roofing. The museum is set up on concrete pillars to obviate the risk of flooding. It has a glazed entry zone and sky-lit first-floor galleries. The boat halls have access doors that allow boats to be brought directly inside. Touching once again on a theme that is a recurring one in his work, Chipperfield's office states that "by negotiating the aesthetic sensibilities of rural England, the River & Rowing Museum merges figure and abstraction, appearing behind its screen of poplar trees to reveal both convention and invention."

Above:
The lobby of the museum

Opposite:
The southern façade has transparent glass walls with stainless-steel trims and retractable fabric sun shades

Right:
An early sketch

1996–2002 ▸ Private House in Corrubedo

Galicia, Spain

Above:
Site plan

Opposite:
The façade of the house that faces the ocean

Below:
The house (right) forms part of a thin ribbon of buildings along the seafront

David Chipperfield designed this 210-square-meter private house for a site on the main street of a small fishing village, located on Spain's northwestern Atlantic coast. Contrary to other houses built along the harbor, this residence seeks to make the most of the views available, orienting inside spaces toward the ocean. As the architects describe the project: "From the sea, the collection of individual and apparently random buildings in Corrubedo form a kind of village elevation—a thin ribbon of buildings that, although made up of houses of varying heights and geometries, still presents itself as a unified and solid arrangement. The introduction of a new house with different priorities had to take into consideration its place within this wall. Looking to provide a sense of continuity, the house sits on a solid stone and concrete base, while its upper mass, like the neighboring houses, is punctured by small windows. Placed like a shelf between these two conditions, a large panoramic window, extending the full width of the house, provides all encompassing views across the beach and harbor." Bedrooms located on the lowest level open directly onto the beach, while the kitchen and living spaces are on the first floor. Two further bedrooms are perched on the second floor, beneath a study and an enclosed rooftop terrace, which are at the top of the house. With its sand-colored base reflecting the rocks on the beach, the house assumes a whiter appearance and a more angled geometry as it rises. The architect succeeds both in integrating the house into what appears to be a hodgepodge of different structures along the harbor and, at the same time, in creating an obviously new and exciting form. The house represents an intriguing combination of contextual integration with affirmed modernity.

2001–03 · Gormley Studio

London, UK

Above:
Large central studio space

Opposite:
The upper floors at either end of the studio connect to the ground floor and courtyard via external staircases

Below:
Concept sketch

This workshop and studio for one of England's best known sculptors, Antony Gormley, is located north of the Kings Cross rail station in London, in a predominantly industrial area. The artist required space that was at once big enough to accommodate his largest works and yet retained a certain intimacy. He had worked in a converted laundry building since 1988, but here he obtained three times more space. Gormley, winner of the 1994 Turner Prize, is known for his 20-meter-high weathering steel sculpture, *Angel of the North*, set on a hill near the A1 motorway at Gateshead. With 1000 square meters of gross floor area, the structure "reflects the large-scale, industrial-architectural vernacular of the surrounding buildings." Pitched roofs allowing for ample overhead natural light and galvanized steel stairways define the structure, where interior whiteness and minimal design seem, above all, to form an appropriate, evenly lit environment in which the artist's creative process can develop without distraction. The building provides for an ample yard large enough for truck deliveries and is, in general, designed to the scale of the heavy materials used by the sculptor. Functionally and aesthetically, the Gormley Studio is an exemplary instance of effective collaboration between an architect and an artist. The artist sought space that was particularly suited to his needs but he also expected the architect to transcend the utilitarian, a hope fully met by David Chipperfield.

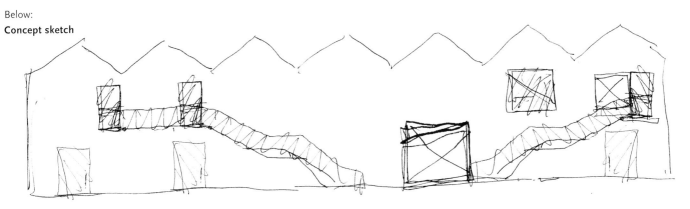

2002–06 ▸ Des Moines Public Library

Des Moines, Iowa, USA

Above:
Concept sketch

Opposite:
External views. The façade is clad in insulating glass with a copper-mesh interleaf

Right:
Aerial view showing the sedum green roof

This two-story concrete structure is clad in a composite glass-metal skin, made with copper mesh set between the outer panes of the triple glazing. The mesh serves to reduce solar gain while allowing visitors to continually see out. In fact, the bookshelves are aligned so that users generally face the exterior. The slight irregularities in the cladding "provide the library with a differentiated yet uniform skin, emphasizing the organic shape of the building." From the outside, the mesh gives a warm metallic orange sheen. Seen in plan, the structure might bring to mind a bird in flight or an aircraft, but its green roof makes it blend into the broad grassy band that it terminates at the eastern end of the park. Built above an underground car park, it has a gross floor area of 13520 square meters. Part of the Western Gateway Park project, an urban renewal scheme for the capital of the state of Iowa that also includes the Pappajohn Sculpture Park opened in 2009 and the Temple for Performing Arts, the Des Moines Public Library does not share with other Chipperfield projects a close proximity to very old buildings, but it does link an urban environment to a greener one. The architect clearly imagined the structure as forming a gateway between the park and the city, with such spaces as the Gateway Gallery, an activity space that is part of a public route through the structure. Education areas, spaces for children, a conference wing, and cafeteria are part of the complex.

2002–06 ▸ Museum of Modern Literature

Marbach am Neckar, Germany

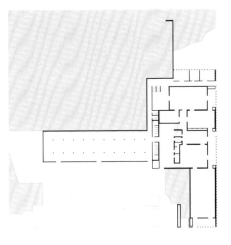

Inaugurated in June 2006, this 3800-square-meter museum is located in Marbach, the birthplace of Friedrich Schiller, and overlooks the Neckar River. Offering panoramic views of the landscape, the structure is embedded in its topography, and makes full use of the steep slope of the site near the Schiller National Museum, which was built in 1903, and the 1970s German Literature Archive. A pavilion-like volume on the uppermost level marks the entrance to the museum, leading down toward dark timber-paneled exhibition galleries. In the galleries, only artificial light is used, given the light-sensitivity of books or works on paper. At the same time, each of these environmentally controlled spaces borders onto a naturally lit gallery, so as to balance views inward to the composed, internalized world of texts and manuscripts with the green and scenic valley on the other side of the glass. As is often the case, the office uses sober materials—such as fair-faced concrete, sandblasted precast concrete elements with limestone aggregate for the façades, limestone, wood, felt, and glass—to give the solid, modern feeling that it masters so well. Among other awards, the museum won the Stirling Prize in 2007.

Above:
Lower ground-floor plan showing the exhibition spaces of the new building

Opposite:
Exhibition level

Right:
Open loggia, entrance level

Next spread:
View from the valley. The Museum of Modern Literature with the adjacent Schiller National Museum

2005–06 ▸ America's Cup Building "Veles e Vents"

Valencia, Spain

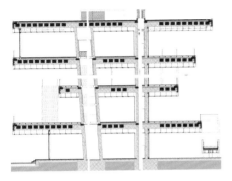

Above:
Section drawing

Opposite:
View along the waterfront during the America's Cup event with spectators on the building's viewing decks

In June 2005, David Chipperfield Architects won the competition to design the "Veles e Vents" building and accompanying park for the Spanish venue of the America's Cup in June 2005. The building was completed just 11 months later in May 2006. The 2007 America's Cup race had a particular resonance because it corresponded to the first European presence of the event in more than a century and a half. Team Alinghi from Switzerland chose Valencia as the location for the race after they defeated Team New Zealand in 2003. The 10 000-square-meter structure and accompanying parking area were intended for the teams themselves and their sponsors, but also for public viewing on decks that extend from the building. The structure includes four stories and is made up of a series of "stacked and overlapping horizontal planes that provide shade and uninterrupted views out to sea." The most visible aspect of the architecture as seen from the exterior is, indeed, that of the concrete slabs that are cantilevered as much as 15 meters over each other, an effect achieved with a hollow concrete floor design. David Chipperfield Architects collaborated in this instance with Fermín Vázquez b720 Arquitectos and with the well-known Belgian landscape architects Wirtz International. The building has a ground-floor reception zone and VIP facilities, including a public restaurant and bar facing the water. Retail space, another bar, and a viewing platform are situated on the first floor, with VIP facilities, a restaurant, lounge, and wellness center reserved to participants in the event on the second and third levels. White is the dominant color of the design with white metal panels for the ceilings, white resin floors, and steel trim that is painted white on the outside concrete. Solid wood decking is also a feature of the building for the outside flooring of the decks. The project won the Royal Institute of British Architects European Award in 2007.

2001–07 ▸ BBC Scotland at Pacific Quay

Glasgow, UK

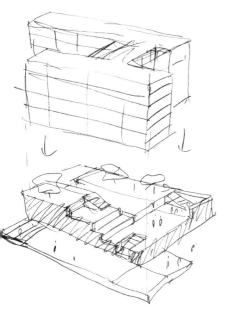

Above:
An early sketch

Opposite:
The central atrium with stepped blocks

Right:
External view from the northeast

This 30 000-square-meter building is located next to the Clyde and Glasgow's former docks. A central atrium was the architectural response to the need to create interaction between people from different divisions of the firm. Areas for television, radio, Internet, production facilities, digital studios, technical support, and office space are all part of the program for the building. Locally quarried red sandstone was used for the steps and terraces within the atrium, an unexpected inversion of materials that apparently makes the studios into elegant stone blocks that step up through the atrium. All of the studios, of varying height, are arranged within the atrium and the offices are arrayed around them. This solution allowed the architects to resolve the problems of difference of scale without undue complexity in the design, while at the same time technical spaces were not undervalued in the sense of being cut off from the rest of the life of the building. The configuration also allowed the creation of opaque studio spaces in close proximity to the more transparent offices. The building has a double-skin glass façade, whose inner surfaces are operable, benefiting from a natural ventilation system between the layers. The façade is generously glazed, offering views of the water. Seen from the exterior, the building is quite strict, as is confirmed by the rectangular plan and main elevation. The real surprise here is reserved to the central atrium.

2003–07 · Am Kupfergraben 10 Gallery Building

Berlin, Germany

The 2000-square-meter building faces Museum Island, where David Chipperfield Architects has ongoing work. Set on the Kupfergraben Canal on the site of a building destroyed during World War II, it also overlooks the Lustgarten. Despite its modern appearance, with a structure made out of reinforced concrete and façades clad in salvaged brick masonry and reconstituted stone, as well as large glass openings with timber framing, the structure respects the scale and alignments of neighboring buildings, much as the office did in its more recent Joachimstrasse offices (see page 84). An upper-floor window is notched to offer a view of a pilaster in the neighboring building. The views of the city from within the Gallery Building are meant to be seen "as if they are part of the art collection." Interior side-lit gallery rooms are no less than 5.5 meters high, with a simple floor plan deployed on four levels. "It is a townhouse dedicated to the arts, not isolated from the world but directly related to the cultural heart of the city."

Above:
Concept sketch

Opposite:
Façade facing the Kupfergraben canal

Right:
Second-floor exhibition room

2004–08 ▸ Ninetree Village

Hangzhou, China

Hangzhou is located in eastern China. It is the capital and largest city of Zhejiang Province. The residential development is framed by a bamboo forest on three sides and is near the Qiantang River. Entry is gained from the south. Twelve residential buildings, each containing five full-floor apartments of about 450 square meters in size, are arranged in order to create a maximum amount of open space around each structure. There are six building types articulated to obtain the best available light and views. An oiled wooden screen of varying density that recalls some traditional Chinese design solutions covers the buildings, providing privacy for the residents. Loggia areas around the structures provide a transition between exterior and interior. Interior materials range from local volcanic stone for public or general areas to natural stone, oiled wood, silk, and lacquer for private spaces.

Above:
Site plan

Opposite:
Garden spaces surround and unite the twelve buildings

Right:
A living room opening into the bamboo garden

49

ES SCHUF PROMETHEUS JEDE KUNST
DEN STERBLICHEN.

1997–2009 ▸ Neues Museum
Museum Island, Berlin, Germany

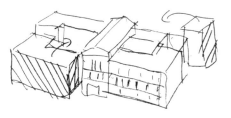

Above:
Concept sketch

Opposite:
**Room of the Niobids, view towards
North Dome Room**

Below:
Section through the east wing

Next spread:
**View from the colonnaded courtyard
towards the Neues Museum**

In 1997, David Chipperfield Architects (in collaboration with Julian Harrap) won the international competition to rebuild the Neues Museum on Berlin's Museum Island. The significance of this commission cannot be overestimated; Museum Island is in many senses at the heart of German culture. Designed by Friedrich August Stüler (1841–59), the Neues Museum was heavily damaged during World War II. The architects state: "The key aim of the project was to recomplete the original volume, and encompassed the repair and restoration of the parts that remained after the destruction of World War II. The original sequence of rooms was restored with new building sections that create continuity with the existing structure." David Chipperfield Architects conscientiously filled the gaps left by war and followed the guidelines of the Charter of Venice, "respecting the historical structure in its different states of preservation." Prefabricated concrete elements were used to create new exhibition rooms and the staircase. Recycled, handmade bricks were used in other new volumes, including the Northwest Wing and the South Dome. As surprising as the use of a strictly designed concrete staircase in a 19th-century building might be to some, the architects' recourse to such materials is justified by his determination to see to it that "the new reflects the lost without imitating it." Though somewhat controversial, partly because it renders permanent certain scars of the war, Chipperfield's approach to this museum, intended

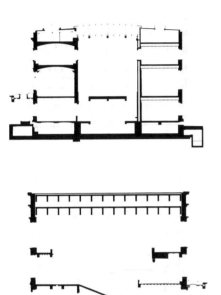

Above:
Sections through the Egyptian Courtyard and the Staircase Hall

Opposite:
Greek Courtyard

Right:
Staircase Hall. The staircase follows the form but not the details of the destroyed stairway it replaces

for the display of Egyptian antiquities, among other things, seems to be very appropriate and successful. The exhibition design for this 20 500-square-meter project was carried out with the collaboration of Michele De Lucchi. The Neues Museum received numerous prestigious awards, including the 2011 European Union Prize for Contemporary Architecture—Mies van der Rohe Award. The citation reads in part: "A prize for conservation was presented to the Neues Museum, Berlin, for the manner in which this badly damaged building was restored and given a new lease of life. The marks of damage have not been covered up, but have been embedded into the new structure and old and new architecture are linked through a magnificent rebuilding scheme that was overseen by the English architect David Chipperfield." Elaborating on his reflections concerning "ordinariness" in contemporary architecture, David Chipperfield states: "I suppose I am really interested in the fact that, in the end, a building should have a continuous dynamic, an internal dynamic relationship with itself, and I think that is why the Neues Museum is probably the most extreme representation of that... The idea is that the project is held together by a singular vision... My ambition is towards coherence. It has to do with a singularity and of course in the Neues Museum, trying to get that coherence from a ruin of a million fragments was probably the most complex idea."[1]

1 David Chipperfield, quoted in *El Croquis* 150, "David Chipperfield, 2006–2010," Madrid, 2010.

Above:
Ethnographic Room before, during, and after restoration

Opposite:
Staircase Hall and Modern Room

Below:
Archaeological Promenade

David Chipperfield is involved in the ongoing master plan for Museum Island. After the Neues Museum, this project is continuing with an entirely new building, the James Simon Gallery (2007–17). This new entrance building is being erected between the Neues Museum and the Spree, "echoing the urban situation of the site pre-1938." The new structure will seek to extend and amplify the idea of a colonnade that existed on Museum Island, while permitting the creation of modern facilities for visitors. This structure and the Archeological Promenade form the spine of the overall master plan. The Archeological Promenade creates a link between the museums and provides further space for the archeological collections. The building is named after Henri James Simon (1851–1932), who donated more than 10 000 objects to the Berlin State Museums, including the bust of Nefertiti that is a centerpiece of the restored Neues Museum. The James Simon Gallery will house temporary exhibition space, an auditorium, a ticket office, gift shop, café, restaurant, and an information center.

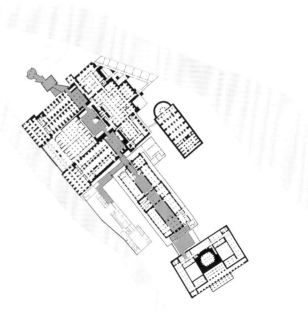

2002–11 ▸ City of Justice

Barcelona and L'Hospitalet de Llobregat, Spain

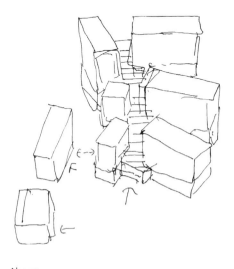

Replacing offices formerly dispersed in 17 separate buildings, this nine-building complex offers 241 500 square meters of gross floor area. Carried out for GISA, Departament de Justícia (Generalitat de Catalunya), the project was carried forward with the assistance of Fermín Vázquez b720 Arquitectos. Four of the new buildings, with courtrooms on the ground floor and offices above, are linked by a continuous four-story concourse, and, on the whole, the design "attempts to break the rigid and monolithic image of justice." The black-and-white concourse has glass and woven mesh facing. Aside from this judiciary core, the complex includes a forensic sciences building, two commercial structures with ground-floor retail areas, and finally a court services building serving L'Hospitalet. The complex is set at the juncture of Barcelona and L'Hospitalet de Llobregat, and also includes a 10th building, for social housing. Despite their differentiation in terms of function and location, the buildings all have load-bearing poured-in-place concrete façades, with slightly different, subdued colors.

Above:
Concept sketch

Opposite:
External view from the surrounding plaza

Below:
View across the site from the south

2003–09 ▸ Anchorage Museum at Rasmuson Center

Anchorage, Alaska, USA

Above:
Concept sketch

Opposite, top:
View of the western extension through the new landscaped public park

Opposite, bottom:
View from the north

Below:
View across Anchorage with the Chugach Mountains in the background

In a very different context, half the world away, in 2009, David Chipperfield completed a new 8400-square-meter expansion of the Anchorage Museum in Alaska. As opposed to the cultural and historic density of Berlin, Anchorage grew almost accidentally from the choice of the site of a railroad construction port for the Alaska Railroad in 1914. The architect chose to compose the new structure from a total of five blocks of varying heights and lengths set along the western side of the existing building. Facing downtown Anchorage, the building creates a new entrance to the museum. Despite being markedly different in appearance from neighboring buildings, the expansion clearly fits into the volumetric disposition of the area, while also reflecting the mountainous landscape in the distance. An open park space in front of the structure offers a new public area to the city. The striped mirror pattern of the glass façades allows the building to be reflective in the context of its neighborhood and also affords views of the exterior to visitors inside. The interior includes an entrance lobby, circulation atrium, café, and exhibition spaces, with different colors and materials used "to give each its own identity." The building houses the Smithsonian Arctic Studies Center, with 600 Alaska Native ethnographic artifacts from the Smithsonian Institution's National Museum of Natural History and National Museum of the American Indian. With its concrete and glass design, laid out in a strictly rectilinear pattern, the Anchorage Museum Expansion surely has a certain coldness that is perhaps justified by the environment, but that is also in some sense typical of the work of David Chipperfield Architects.

2006–10 ▸ Laboratory Building

Basel, Switzerland

Above:
West elevation

Opposite:
Façade detail, south elevation

Below:
Open garden courtyard with permanent installation _Molecular (BASEL)_ by Serge Spitzer

Built for Novartis Pharma, this 11 600-square-meter (first phase) building is part of the larger Novartis campus in Basel, which will include 22 new buildings by architects such as Fumihiko Maki, Diener & Diener, Frank Gehry, and SANAA, based on a master plan by Vittorio Magnago Lampugnani. The master plan determines such elements as building and ground-floor heights. David Chipperfield Architects designed a five-story laboratory building at the center of the campus with a central open courtyard facing Fabrikstrasse. The northern and eastern wings of the Chipperfield complex are due for construction in the second phase. Given the desire of the client to benefit from a maximum degree of flexibility in the laboratory floors, a supporting structure was developed which allows for a column-free floor plan. This was achieved by a load-bearing façade made with precast concrete units and beams that span 27 meters between two building cores and integrate the technical conduits. Full-height glazing allows for natural light to enter all the workspaces. One unusual feature of the project is a three-story yellow staircase connecting the laboratory levels to the top-floor offices designed by Ross Lovegrove. An art installation by Serge Spitzer is located in the garden, which is enclosed by the fifth (top) level of the building. The building received a 2011 RIBA International Award. The jury verdict reads in part: "The colonnade is a recurring theme in David Chipperfield's architecture and here it adds a classical seriousness to this laboratory of the future for the pharmaceutical company Novartis; it also picks up on the use of the device in neighboring buildings."

2007–10 ▸ Folkwang Museum

Essen, Germany

Above:
Site plan

Opposite, top:
Permanent exhibition

Opposite, bottom:
East façade, view from Bismarckstrasse

Below:
Section

The Folkwang Museum, founded in Hagen by Karl Ernst Osthaus in 1902, was Europe's first museum of contemporary art, showing work from artists like Ernst Ludwig Kirchner, Emil Nolde, Aristide Maillol and Henri Matisse. The most significant works were transferred from Hagen to Essen in 1922, and today it is one of Germany's highest profile art museums. In 2007, David Chipperfield Architects won the international competition for an extension to the museum. The opening of the extension was timed to coincide with the tenure of Essen and the Ruhr region as European Capital of Culture. A composition of six structures and four inner courtyards, offering an additional 3600 square meters of exhibition space, complements the original building and preserves its integrity. David Chipperfield Architects created a "translucent, alabaster-like façade consisting of large rectangular recycled glass slabs." Transparent windows are inserted, flush with the rest of the glass façade. Galleries with polished screed floors offer ceiling heights up to six meters. The 24 800-square-meter structure includes a library, reading room, multifunctional hall, and an events space, as well as storage and restoration areas. Strict and functional in its appearance, the Folkwang Museum extension succeeds in creating a kind of shimmering presence that fits in well with Chipperfield's avowed interest in being at the edge of "ordinariness" and "specialness."

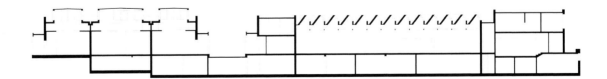

2007–10 ▸ Kaufhaus Tyrol Department Store

Innsbruck, Austria

In this instance, David Chipperfield Architects has sought to integrate a rather powerful and clearly modern 58000-square-meter building into the historic context of the center of Innsbruck. The new building occupies the space of the former Kaufhaus Tyrol and stretches from Maria-Theresien-Strasse through the interior of the block, with its central atrium through to Erlerstrasse. In an unexpected way, the three sections of the main façade, which are set at a slight angle to each other, do succeed in taking up the rhythm of the old street. The strongly articulated, precast-concrete façade elements make way for deeply set, room-height windows that also participate in the integration of the new building into the city's spirit in terms of light and shadow, as well as the dimensions of neighboring building surfaces. Emphasizing the effort made to blend into the city without sacrificing the fundamentals of modernity, the architects state: "The neighboring Schindlerhaus, dating back to the 16th century, has been carefully restored and a new floor added, providing space for offices and meeting rooms and for the former Schindler Café." Despite all of this attention to history, it comes as no surprise that the interior of the Kaufhaus Tyrol contains a five-story, naturally lit atrium offering central access to all the floors. The architects have clearly mastered the method and substance of building in the old city center of Innsbruck.

Above:
The interior of the mall with the main escalator

Opposite:
Maria-Theresien-Strasse, view from the south

Right:
Erlerstrasse, view from the north

2006–11 ▸ Turner Contemporary

Margate, UK

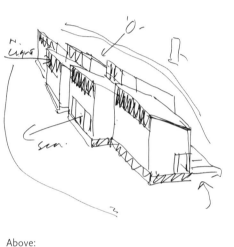

Above:
Concept sketch

Opposite:
Turner Contemporary (right) seen from the harbor of Margate

Right:
The building sits on the waterfront, overlooking the North Sea

Located in Margate, on the north coast of Kent in southern England, Turner Contemporary is made up of six identical, interconnected "crystalline" volumes with a concrete frame, and mono-pitched roofs angled to bring northern light into the upper-floor galleries. Warmer southern light is admitted through diffused roof lights in the angled ceilings of the galleries, resulting in natural light without shadows. The architects refer to a "cluster of large sheds" in describing the design, and the exterior appearance of the building is, indeed, quite simple. Turner Contemporary opened to the public in 2011. More a *kunsthalle* than a museum, Turner Contemporary does not have its own permanent collection but places an emphasis, instead, on the work of J. M. W. Turner (1775–1851) through historic and contemporary works. It is located near the water on the site of a former car park and a guesthouse where the great painter stayed. With a gross floor area of 3100 square meters, the building has an almost ghostly presence on the beachfront. The ground floor includes a reception area, event space, and a café. Set near the water, the building is raised on a plinth to obviate the effects of occasional flooding. The acid-etched reinforced-glass-skin façades were designed "to withstand the corrosive nature of the sea, high humidity levels, strong winds, and the occasional wave overtopping the building." An outdoor terrace extends the public space of the complex during warmer months.

Opposite, top:
View into the ground-floor event space through large windows on the north side

Opposite, bottom:
View out to sea from the entrance area

Below:
First-floor gallery space

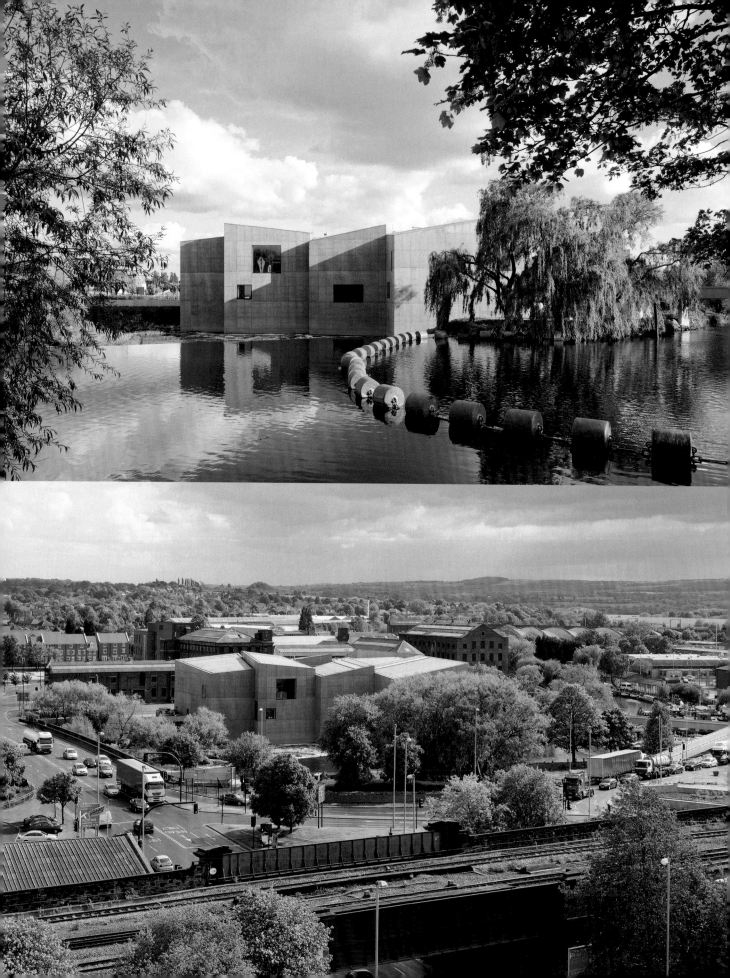

2003–11 ▶ The Hepworth Wakefield

Wakefield, UK

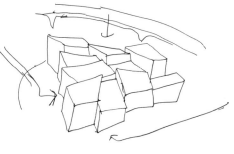

Above:
Concept sketch

Opposite, top:
View from the bank of the River Calder

Opposite, bottom:
Aerial view showing the building

Right:
First-floor gallery space

Next spread:
View from north

The Hepworth Wakefield is named after the noted modern sculptor Dame Barbara Hepworth, who was born in Wakefield in 1903, and died in 1975. The purpose-built 5230-square-meter art gallery is located on the bank of the River Calder in the Wakefield Waterfront Conservation area, former home to the city's cloth and grain industries. Given the nature of the site, the structure has no dominant façade. The architects state: "The almost geological composition is a conglomerate of diverse irregular forms tightly fitting one another. This form was driven by the internal program and organization of the gallery." In plan, the structure is clearly formed by a series of nestled, irregular blocks that fit together in a coherent way. As seen from the exterior, the building retains a certain irregularity emphasized by the differing angles of the roofs of each block. Pigmented in-situ concrete was used, giving a "monolithic appearance" to the building. The ground floor contains the reception area, a shop, cafeteria, auditorium, learning studios, and offices. A central stairway leads to the upper-level galleries that have open doorways and a "fluid and varied sequence." Daylight enters through incisions in the blocks.

2009–13 ▸ Museo Jumex

Mexico City, Mexico

Above:
Concept sketch

Opposite:
View from the northeast of the site. The museum is surrounded by an eclectic mixture of buildings

Below:
Ground-floor entrance area with large doors opening onto the public plaza and the cafeteria

The Museo Jumex was built on a triangular site in the Polanco area of Mexico City for the exhibition of one of the largest private collections of contemporary art in Latin America. The architects state: "The building can be described as a freestanding pavilion that corresponds to the eclectic nature of the neighboring buildings, which include the Soumaya Museum (Fernando Romero) and the underground Cervantes Theater (Antón García-Abril)." The design corresponds to the constraints imposed by the program and local planning rules, including the maximum allowed footprint. Given that the client's foundation has maintained its administration, storage facilities, library, and exhibition areas at existing premises in Ecatepec, the new 4000-square-meter building is intended in good part for temporary shows and exhibition of the Jumex collection. The primary exhibition space is on the upper floors, where natural overhead light is available. The architects state: "Consisting of a steel structure with west-facing roof lights and a horizontal diffuser layer, the roof distributes light evenly to illuminate the artworks and create an ambient light for the space." The plinth, 14 columns, ground- and first-floor cores, and the soffits are made of exposed white concrete, while the façades, the roof, and the floors from the plinth upwards are clad in travertine marble from Xalapa, Veracruz. Full-height glazing is set in stainless-steel frames.

Above:
**Second-floor gallery space displaying the work
of James Lee Byars**

Right:
Large top-floor gallery space

Opposite, top:
First-floor multifunction space

Opposite, bottom:
First-floor publicly accessible loggia

2005–13 ▸ Saint Louis Art Museum

St. Louis, Missouri, USA

Above:
Site plan

Opposite, top:
View of the East Building from the southwest

Opposite, bottom:
Entrance to the East Building

Below:
Longitudinal section

The Saint Louis Art Museum is located in the city's 5.5-square-kilometer Forest Park. The original and main building designed by Cass Gilbert was designed as one of the exhibition pavilions for the 1904 St. Louis World's Fair. In 1909, it became the City Art Museum. Extensions and renovations were carried out in the 1950s, 1980, and 1985. David Chipperfield Architects' new East Building is a single-story, 9000-square-meter structure that seeks to keep "its visual impact on the immediate surroundings and its wider environment to a minimum." Erected on a low plinth, the floor level is the same as that of the main floor of the older Cass Gilbert building. Used for the modern and contemporary art collection of the museum, the East Building also provides temporary exhibition spaces, a museum shop, and a significant dining space. Landscaping around the building offers a forecourt, and sculpture gardens that are blended into Forest Park. Dark concrete-paneled façades were cast and polished on site. A coffered concrete ceiling allows modulated natural light into the building. Three hundred parking spaces are part of the project.

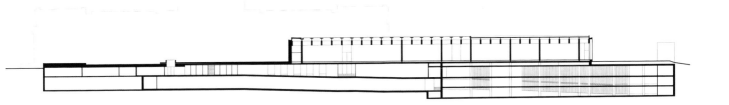

Above and opposite:
Views of the day-lit gallery spaces

2007–13 ▸ Joachimstrasse

Berlin, Germany

Located in the district of Mitte, the site occupies a deep plot in an urban block that was heavily damaged during World War II. The surrounding area is a dense mixture of historic and prefabricated concrete buildings. Built as the Berlin offices of the architects, this complex is made with monolithic walls of insulating concrete. The architects have added four concrete structures to an existing brick building for a gross floor area of 1800 square meters. The residential front building with exhibition spaces and function rooms closes the street façade and its overall proportions respond to the neighboring structures. Two cubic blocks of different heights were added in the middle of the plot, conserving a sense of a typical prewar courtyard design. A two-story volume serves as a canteen. The taller four-story structure in the center of the complex provides meeting rooms and is directly linked to the older building. Large windows, which are offset at each story, provide diverse views in, out, and through the buildings, varying the simple stacked floor plan. The interior finishes are reduced with polished screed flooring, timber, and marble.

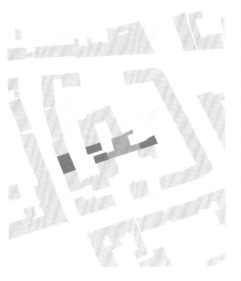

Above:
Site plan

Opposite:
Middle buildings, view from the second courtyard

Right:
Front house, view from Joachimstrasse

Next spread:
View from the first courtyard. Middle house extension (right) and the canteen (left)

2008– ▸ Naqa Museum

Naqa, Sudan

Above:
Exhibition Hall showing the indirect natural lighting and the muted coloring of the design

Opposite:
West elevation of the structure as it will appear in its desert setting

Below:
Concept sketch

Located 170 kilometers northeast of Khartoum and 50 kilometers from the Nile, the Unesco World Heritage Site Naqa is a former religious center dating from the Meroitic Empire (ca. 300 B.C.–300 A.D.). Two notable temples devoted to Amun and Apedemak stand in this location, otherwise marked only by an artesian well, a watchhouse, and a temporary archeologists' building. Naqa can be reached only via sand tracks, after a three-hour drive from the capital. Working with Dietrich Wildung of the Egyptian Museum of Berlin, David Chipperfield Architects has designed a low 1400-square-meter building to store the archeologist's finds on site. Slightly stepped, the building is to be close to the Temple of Amun. Compressed concrete made with local sand and aggregates will form the outer walls of the structure, while a prefabricated roof will allow light into the building, which contains an arrival loggia, a ramp, courtyard, and exhibition space. No glass is employed in the design, and, as the architects make clear, it is "designed first and foremost to provide protection from sun, rain, and looting." When David Chipperfield speaks of this project, he does so with an evident passion. He is clearly fascinated by the challenges of building in such a difficult location, and with a minimal budget. He is also taken with the questions posed by the desert environment, and in particular the potentially devastating effects of sand, light, and heat. This may be a simple structure in many respects, but its location and function render it quite complex to realize. Few designers of the notoriety of Chipperfield might accept to undertake such a commission and his involvement is indicative of his real passion for architecture.

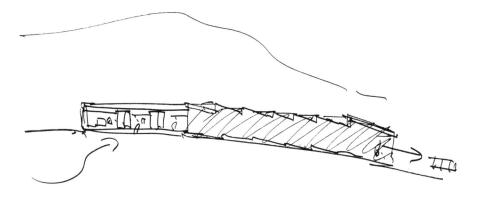

2010–▸ Amorepacific Headquarters

Seoul, South Korea

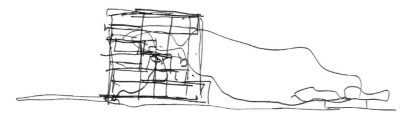

This headquarters building for the Korean cosmetics company Amorepacific is located in the center of Seoul, and has a substantial gross floor area of 216000 square meters. The architects state: "The primary aim for the project was to create a building with a distinct identity within a highly diverse urban context. The massing of the building therefore focuses on a single, clear volume with an inner courtyard as its centre, avoiding similarities with the surrounding iconographic towers. Large openings in the façade with elevated gardens connect the building with the city and the adjacent park, creating a dialogue between architecture and nature." The external appearance of the structure is defined by a double skin consisting of full-height glazing covered by external aluminum fins. These vertical fins have a slightly irregular placement that enlivens the exterior appearance of the building. The appearance of the façades also brings to mind traditional Asian screens. Interior areas are made with poured-in-place concrete, glass, and natural stone. In addition to the office space, the program provides for a museum, auditorium and conference space, restaurants, and some retail areas, located around the atrium lobby in the lower part of the building.

Top:
Concept sketch

Above:
Courtyard formed by the volumes of the building

Opposite:
Southeast elevation, view from the park

Right:
The atrium with its generous volume and natural lighting

London office:
Rik Nys, Louise Dier, Oliver Ulmer,
and Billy Prendergast

Berlin office:
Harald Müller, Christoph Felger, Eva Schad,
Martin Reichert, and Alexander Schwarz

Milan office: Giuseppe Zampieri
Shanghai office: Libin Chen and Mark Randel

World Map

Project Teams

Toyota Auto Kyoto *Team*: Jorge Carvalho, Jan Coghlan, Jamie Fobert, Spencer Fung, Michael Greville, Naoko Kawamura, Cecilia Lau, Haruo Morishima, Ko Nakatani, Toshiki Wakisaka, Sarah Wong

Private House in Berlin *Team*: Philipp Auer, Brigitte Becker, Stevan Brown, Jamie Fobert, Mark Randel, Eva Schad, Mia Schlegel, Mechthild Stuhlmacher, Henning Stummel

River & Rowing Museum *Team*: Renato Benedetti, Peter Crompton, Rebecca Elliot, Spencer Fung, Alec Gillies, Victoria Jessen-Pike, Harvey Langston-Jones, Genevieve Lilley, Andrew Llowarch, Rik Nys, John Onken, Peter Andreas Sattrup, Silvana Schulze, Maurice Shapiro, Mechthild Stuhlmacher, Simon Timms

Private House in Corrubedo *Team*: Louise Brooker, Luca Donadoni, Pablo Gallego Picard, Ricardo Iboim Inglés, Victoria Jessen-Pike, Daniel López-Pérez, Carlos Martínez de Albornoz, Tina Sophie Müller, Anat Talmor, Oliver Ulmer, Giuseppe Zampieri

Gormley Studio *Team*: Kevin Carmody, Andy Groarke, Kaori Ohsugi

Des Moines Public Library *Team*: Doreen Bernath, Franz Borho, Martin Ebert, Chris Hardie, Victoria Jessen-Pike, Ilona Klockenbusch, Hartmut Kortner, Michael Kruse, Kaori Ohsugi, Kim Wang, Reiko Yamazaki

Museum of Modern Literature *Partners*: Alexander Schwarz (Design director) Harald Müller (Managing director); *Project architect*: Martina Betzold; *Team*: Laura Fogarasi, Andrea Hartmann, Christian Helfrich, Hannah Jonas, Barbara Koller, Franziska Rusch, Tobias Stiller, Vincent Taupitz, Mirjam von Busch

America's Cup Building "Veles e Vents" *Team*: Marco de Battista, Mirja Giebler, Jochen Glemser, Regina Gruber, David Gutman, Andrew Phillips, Melissa Johnston

BBC Scotland at Pacific Quay *Team*: Gabrielle Allam, Johannes Baumstark, Kevin Carmody, Mario Cottone, Paul Crosby, Martin Ebert, David Finlay, Robin Foster, Andy Groarke, Manuel Gujber, Victoria Jessen-Pike, Kaori Ohsugi, Billy Prendergast, Hau Ming Tse, Oliver Ulmer, Jonathan Wong, Toni Yli-Suvanto, Giuseppe Zampieri

Am Kupfergraben 10 Gallery Building *Partners*: Alexander Schwarz (Design director), Harald Müller (Managing director); *Project architect*: Barbara Koller; *Team*: Martina Betzold, Laura Fogarasi, Andrea Hartmann, Hannah Jonas, Elke Saleina

Ninetree Village *Partner*: Mark Randel; *Project architect*: Hans Krause; *Team*: Christoph Bartscherer, Libin Chen, Ulrich Hannen, Christian Helfrich, Lijun Shen, Natalia Vinuela

Neues Museum *Partners*: Alexander Schwarz (Design director), Harald Müller, Martin Reichert, Eva Schad (Managing directors); *Project architects*: Mark Randel (competition), Martin Reichert, Eva Schad; *Team*: Thomas Benk (Team leader historic constructions), Katja Buchholz, Nils Dallmann, Florian Dirschedl, Maryla Duleba, Matthias Fiegl, Annette Flohrschütz, Michael Freytag (Team leader new construction), Anke Fritzsch (Team leader restoration), Anne Hengst, Michael Kaune, Regine Krause, Paul Ludwig, Marcus Mathias, Max Ott, Peter Pfeiffer, Martina Pongratz, Robert Ritzmann, Mariska Rohde, Franziska Rusch, Elke Saleina, Sonia Sandberger, Antonia Schlegel, Lukas Schwind

City of Justice *Team*: Gabrielle Allam, Motohisa Arai, Tomomi Araki, Albert Arraut, Alex Bauer, Johannes Baumstark, Doreen Bernath, Roberta Buccheri, Christian Clemares, Mario Cottone, Luca Donadoni, Martin Eglin, Massimo Fenati, David Finlay, Pablo Gil, Jochen Glemser, Regina Gruber, Serena Jaff, Victoria Jessen-Pike, Melissa Johnston, Michael Krusse, Reto Liechti, Claudia Lucchini, Alessandra Maiolino, Emanuele Mattutini, Sabrina Melera-Morettini, Takayuki Nakajima, Rentaro Nishimura, Cecilia Obiol, Luca Parmeggiani, Ignacio Peydro, Andrew Phillips, Sashwin Pillai, Simon Pole, John Puttick, Oscar Rodriguez, Anika Scholin, Melanie Schubert, Jordi Sinfreu Alay, Jennifer Singer, Giuseppe Sirica, Cordula Stach, Hau Ming Tse, Patrick Ueberbacher, Laura Vega, Philippe Volpe, Giuseppe Zampieri

Anchorage Museum at Rasmuson Center *Team*: Vesna Aksentijevic, Franz Borho, Pedro Castelo Ferreira, Isabelle Heide, Melissa Johnston, Christian Junge, Mattias Kunz, Peter Kleine, Marina Mitchell-Heggs, Andrew Phillips, Billy Prendergast, Dominik Schwarzer, Robert Steul, Oliver Ulmer

Laboratory Building *Partners*: Alexander Schwarz (Design director), Harald Müller (Managing director); *Project architects*: Christian Helfrich, Robert Westphal; *Team*: Markus Bauer, Lena Ehringhaus, Niccolo Genesio, Gesche Gerber, Ulrich Hannen, Paul Hillerkus, Nicolas Kulemeyer, Astrid Kühn, Sebastian von Oppen, Asa Awad Osman, Martina Pongratz, Stefanie Schleipen, Gunda Schulz

Folkwang Museum *Partners*: Alexander Schwarz (Design director), Harald Müller (Managing director); *Project architects*: Peter von Matuschka (competition), Ulrike Eberhardt, Eberhard Veit; *Team*: Markus Bauer, Florian Dierschedl, Annette Flohrschütz, Gesche Gerber, Christian Helfrich, Barbara Koller, Nicolas Kulemeyer, Dalia Liksaite, Marcus Mathias, Sebastian von Oppen, Ilona Priwitzer, Mariska Rohde, Franziska Rusch, Antonia Schlegel, Marika Schmidt, Thomas Schöpf, Gunda Schulz, Manuel Seebass, Robert Westphal

Kaufhaus Tyrol Department Store *Partners*: Christoph Felger (Design director), Harald Müller (Managing director); *Project architects*: Ulrich Goertz, Hans Krause; *Team*: Florian Dietrich, Kristen Finke, Ole Hallier, Paul Hillerkus, Guido Kappius, Mikhail Kornev, Katrin Löscher, Michael Schmidt, Lukas Schwind, François von Chappuis, Boris Wolf

Turner Contemporary *Director*: Franz Borho; *Project architects*: Holger Mattes, Caroline Rogerson; *Team*: Jennifer Bonner, Yael Brosilovski, Katrin Brünjes, Daniel Buckley, Corina Eberling, Demian Erbar, Jonathan French, Jochen Glemser, Matthias Heberle, Tom Herre, Nick Hill, Silke Hoss, Victoria Jessen-Pike, Akira Kindo, Andrew Phillips, Billy Prendergast, Manuel Shvartzberg, Oliver Ulmer, Steffi Wedde, Reiko Yamazaki

The Hepworth Wakefield *Director*: Oliver Ulmer; *Project architects*: Demian Erbar, Nick Hill, Kelvin Jones; *Team*: Julie Bauer, Yael Brosilovski, Katrin Bruenjes, Jesús Donaire, Corina Ebeling, John Puttick, Claudia Faust, Jason Good, David Gutman, Victoria Jessen-Pike, Ilona Klockenbusch, Daniel Koo, Laurent Masmonteil, Hau Ming Tse, Stephen Molloy, Hiroshi Nagata, Anna Naumann, Sabine Piechotta, Dean Pike, Billy Prendergast, Declan Scullion, Pierre Swanepoel, Korinna Thielen, Steffi Wedde, Jose Bergua

Practice Profile

Museo Jumex *Director*: Andrew Phillips; *Project architect*: Peter Jurschitzka; *Team*: Matt Ball, Jonathan Cohen, Trent Davies, Johannes Feder, Christian Felgendreher, Sara Hengsbach, Alessandro Milani, Diana Su

Saint Louis Art Museum *Director*: Franz Borho; *Project architect*: Julie Bauer; *Team*: Stuart A. Beck, Daniel Buckley, Paul Crosby, Jesús Donaire Garcia de la Mora, Thomas Friberg, Isabella Gerster, David Gutman, Tom Herre, Silke Hoss, Victoria Jessen-Pike, Akira Kindo, Ilona Klockenbusch, Martin Leisi, Nina Lundvall, Rob Liedgens, Marina Mitchell-Heggs, Andrew Phillips, Dominik Schwarzer, Oliver Ulmer, Matti Wirth

Joachimstrasse *Partners*: Alexander Schwarz (Design director), Mark Randel (Managing director), Eva Schad, Harald Müller (Directors representing the client); *Project architects*: Lukas Schwind, Marcus Mathias; *Team*: Ulrike Eberhardt, Gesche Gerber, Sascha Jung, Sandra Morar, Christof Piaskowski, Thomas Schöpf

Naqa Museum *Partners*: Alexander Schwarz (Design director), Martin Reichert (Managing director); *Project architects:* Thomas Benk, Michael Freytag; *Team*: Felix Buschinger, Elisa Giusti, Pascal Maas, Antonia Schlegel

Amorepacific Headquarters *Partners*: Christoph Felger (Design director), Harald Müller (Managing director); *Project architect*: Hans Krause; *Team*: Isabel Albano-Müller, Wolfram Belz, Ivan Dimitrov, Franziska Friebel, Christoph Goeke, Anne Hengst, Matthias Heskamp, Frank Jödicke, Frithjof Kahl, Nicolas Kulemeyer, Anke Lawrence, Ho Sun Lee, Jens Lorbeer, Pascal Maas, Sandra Morar, Diogo Passarinho, Ilona Priwitzer, Thomas Pyschny, Franziska Rusch, Susie Ryu, Noriyuki Sawaya, Diana Schaffrannek, Gunda Schulz, Lijun Shen, Caroline Stahl, Christian Stöckert, Natacha Viveiros, Peter von Matuschka, Robert Westphal

Since its foundation in 1985, David Chipperfield Architects has developed a diverse international body of work including cultural, residential, commercial, leisure and civic projects as well as master-planning exercises. Within the portfolio of museums and galleries, projects range from private collections such as the Museo Jumex in Mexico City to public institutions such as the revitalized Neues Museum in Berlin. Practices in London, Berlin, Milan, and Shanghai contribute to the wide range of projects and typologies.

The practice's work is unified and characterized by meticulous attention to the concept and details of every project, and a relentless focus on refining the design ideas to arrive at a solution which is architecturally, socially, and intellectually coherent. The collaborative aspect of creating architecture is at the heart of every single project from inception to completion.

David Chipperfield Architects has won numerous international awards and citations for design excellence, including the RIBA Stirling Prize in 2007 (for the Museum of Modern Literature in Marbach, Germany), and the European Union Prize for Contemporary Architecture—Mies van der Rohe Award, and the Deutscher Architekturpreis in 2011 (both for the Neues Museum).

David Chipperfield Architects' entire team gathering at the 13th International Exhibition of Architecture in Venice, which was curated by David Chipperfield in 2012

David Chipperfield:
Life and Work

David Chipperfield was Professor of Architecture at the Staatliche Akademie der Bildenden Künste, Stuttgart, from 1995 to 2001 and Norman R. Foster Visiting Professor of Architectural Design at Yale University in 2011, and he has taught and lectured worldwide at schools of architecture in Austria, Italy, Switzerland, the United Kingdom, and the United States. In 2012, David Chipperfield curated the 13th International Architecture Exhibition of the Venice Biennale. In 2014, he was appointed Artistic Director of the Italian furnishings firm Driade.

He is an honorary fellow of both the American Institute of Architects and the Bund Deutscher Architekten, and a past winner of the Heinrich Tessenow Gold Medal, the Wolf Foundation Prize in the Arts, and the Grand DAI (Verband Deutscher Architekten- und Ingenieurvereine) Award for Building Culture. David Chipperfield was appointed Commander of the Order of the British Empire in 2004, appointed a Royal Designer for Industry in 2006, and elected to the Royal Academy in 2008. In 2009, he was awarded the Order of Merit of the Federal Republic of Germany and in 2010 he was knighted for services to architecture in the UK and Germany. In 2011 he received the RIBA Royal Gold Medal for Architecture, and in 2013, the Praemium Imperiale from the Japan Art Association, both given in recognition of a lifetime's work.

Credits

Photographers and Illustrators: 6, 25, 50, 54, 56 © SMB/Ute Zscharnt for David Chipperfield Architects; 7, 11, 14, 17, 18, 44, 47 bottom, 52–53, 62, 63 left, 64 top, 66, 67 left and bottom, 84 © Ute Zscharnt for David Chipperfield Architects; 8, 30, 31 left, 34, 35 left, 69 bottom, 70 bottom © Richard Bryant/Arcaid; 9, 32, 33 bottom © Hélène Binet; 10, 36 © Des Moines Public Library/Farshid Assassi; 12, 13, 22, 28, 37 bottom, 39 bottom, 40–41, 45 bottom, 48, 49 bottom, 58, 59 bottom, 60 top and bottom, 61 bottom, 64 bottom © Christian Richters; 15, 21, 23, 68, 70 top, 71, 76, 77 bottom–80 bottom, 82, 85 bottom, 86–87 © Simon Menges; 26, 27 left © Alberto Piovano; 29 bottom © Stefan Müller; 38, 57 top © Jörg von Bruchhausen; 42 © ACM 2007/Carlos Lujan; 46 © Ioana Marinescu; 55 bottom © SPK/Jörg von Bruchhausen; 63 bottom © Ulrich Schwarz; 72 top and bottom, 73 bottom, 74–75 © Iwan Baan; 82 top © Wesley Law; 83 © Aaron Dougherty; 92 middle © Heinz Jirout for David Chipperfield Architects; 92 bottom right © Yangzhi Feng; 95 © Isabella Balena

The Author

Philip Jodidio studied art history and economics at Harvard, and edited *Connaissance des Arts* for over 20 years. His books include TASCHEN's *Architecture Now!* series, and monographs on Tadao Ando, Norman Foster, Richard Meier, Jean Nouvel, and Zaha Hadid. He is internationally renowned as one of the most popular writers on the subject of architecture.